JAMES BALDWIN
I AM NOT YOUR NEGRO

James Baldwin (1924–1987) was a novelist, essayist, playwright, poet, social critic, and the author of more than twenty books. His first novel, *Go Tell It on the Mountain*, appeared in 1953 to excellent reviews, and his essay collections *Notes of a Native Son* and *The Fire Next Time* were bestsellers that made him an influential figure in the civil rights movement. Baldwin spent many years in France, where he moved to escape the racism and homophobia of the United States. He died in 1987.

Raoul Peck is a filmmaker acclaimed for his historical, political, and artistic work. Born in Haiti, he grew up in Congo, France, Germany, and the United States. His body of work includes the films *The Man by the Shore* (Competition, Cannes 1993); *Lumumba* (Cannes 2000, HBO); and *Sometimes in April* (2005, HBO). He is currently chairman of the French national film school, La Fémis, and recently completed his next feature film, *The Young Karl Marx* (2017).

INTERNATIONAL

ALSO BY JAMES BALDWIN

I AM NOT YOUR NEGRO

I AM NOT YOUR NEGRO

A major motion picture directed by
RAOUL PECK

From texts by
JAMES BALDWIN

compiled and edited by **RAOUL PECK**

VINTAGE INTERNATIONAL
Vintage Books
A Division of Penguin Random House LLC
New York

FIRST VINTAGE INTERNATIONAL EDITION, FEBRUARY 2017

Based on the film I Am Not Your Negro *© 2016 by Velvet Film, Inc. and Velvet Film, SAS*
Compilation and introduction by Raoul Peck © 2017 by Velvet Film, Inc. and Velvet Film, SAS
Introduction by Alexandra Strauss © 2017 by Alexandra Strauss
All quotes and text by James Baldwin © 2017 by The James Baldwin Estate.
Used with permission. All rights reserved.

Grateful acknowledgment is made to Gloria Karefa-Smart
for permission to reprint an excerpt from an unpublished
letter written to Raoul Peck, dated April 2009.

An extension of this copyright page appears on page 115.

The Cataloging-in-Publication Data is on file at the Library of Congress.

Vintage International Trade Paperback ISBN: 978-0-525-43469-6
eBook ISBN: 978-0-525-43471-9

Book design by Christopher M. Zucker

www.vintagebooks.com

Printed in the United States of America
10 9 8 7 6 5 4 3 2 1

CONTENTS

INTRODUCTION
ON A PERSONAL NOTE
by RAOUL PECK

I started reading James Baldwin when I was a fifteen-year-old boy in search of rational explanations for the contradictions I was confronting in my already nomadic life, which would take me from Haiti to Congo to France to Germany and to the United States of America. Together with Aimé Césaire, Jacques Stephen Alexis, Richard Wright, Gabriel García Márquez, and Alejo Carpentier, James Baldwin was one of the few authors I could call "my own." Authors who were speaking of a world I knew, in which I was not just a footnote or a third-rate character. They were telling stories describing history and defining structures and human relationships that matched what I was seeing around me.

I came from a country that had a strong idea of itself, that had fought *and* beaten the most powerful army of the world (Napoléon's), and that had, in a unique historical manner, stopped slavery in its tracks, achieving in 1804 the first successful slave revolution in the history of the world.

I am talking about Haiti, the first free country in the Americas (it is *not*, as commonly believed, the United States of America). Haitians always knew that the dominant story was not the true story.

The successful Haitian Revolution was ignored by history because it imposed a totally different narrative, which rendered the dominant slave narrative of the day untenable.

Deprived of their civilizing justification, the colonial conquests of the late nineteenth century would have been ideologically impossible. And this justification would not have been viable if the world knew that these "savage" Africans had annihilated their powerful armies (especially those of the French and the Spanish) less than a century before.

What the four superpowers of the time did, in an unusually peaceful consensus, was shut down Haiti, the very first black republic, put it under strict economic and diplomatic embargo, and strangle it into poverty and irrelevance.

And then they rewrote the whole story.

Flash forward. I remember my years in New York as a child. A more "civilized" time, I thought. It was the 1960s. In the kitchen of a huge middle-class apartment in a former Jewish neighborhood near Flatbush Avenue in Brooklyn, where we lived with other members of my extended family, a kind of large Oriental rug with images of John F. Kennedy and Martin Luther King, Jr., hung on the wall: the two martyrs, both legends of the time.

Except the revered tapestry was not telling the whole truth. It bluntly ignored the hierarchy between the two figures, the imbalance of power that existed between them. And it thereby nullified any possibility of understanding these two parallel stories that crossed paths for a short time and left in their wake a foggy miasma of misunderstanding.

I grew up inhabiting a myth in which I was both enforcer and actor: the myth of a single and unique America. The script was well written, the soundtrack allowed no ambiguity, the actors of this utopia, whether black or white, were convincing. The production values of this blockbuster were phenomenal. With rare episodic setbacks, the myth was life, was reality. I remember the Kennedys, Bobby and John, and Elvis, Ed Sullivan, Jackie Gleason, Dr. Richard Kimble, and Mary Tyler Moore very well. On the other hand, Otis Redding, Paul Robeson, and Willie Mays are only vague associations, faint stories "tolerated" in my memory's hard disk. Of course there was *Soul Train* on television, but it came much later and aired on Saturday mornings, when it wouldn't offend any advertisers.

Medgar Evers died on June 12, 1963. Malcolm X died on February 21, 1965. And Martin Luther King, Jr., died on April 4, 1968. Over the course of five years, the three men were assassinated.

They were black, but it is not the color of their skin that connected them. They fought on quite different battle-fields. And quite differently. But in the end, all three were deemed dangerous and therefore disposable. For they were eliminating the haze of racial confusion.

Like them, James Baldwin also saw through the system. And he knew and loved these men.

He was determined to expose the complex links and sim-ilarities among Medgar, Malcolm, and Martin. He planned to write about them. He was going to write his ultimate book, *Remember This House*.

I came upon these three men and their assassinations much later. Nevertheless, these three facts, these elements of history, form the starting point, the "evidence" you might say, for a deep and intimate personal reflection on my own political and cultural mythology, my own experiences of racism and intellectual violence.

This is exactly the point when I really needed James Baldwin. Baldwin knew how to deconstruct stories and put them back in their fundamental right order and context. He helped me connect the story of a liberated nation, Haiti, and the story of the modern United States of America and its own painful and bloody legacy of slavery. I could connect the dots.

Baldwin gave me a voice, gave me the words, gave me the rhetoric. At his funeral, Toni Morrison said, "You gave me a language to dwell in, a gift so perfect it seems my own invention." All I knew or had learned through instinct or through experience, Baldwin gave a name to and a shape. I now had all the intellectual ammunition I needed.

For sure, we still have strong winds pummeling us. The present time of discord, ignorance, and confusion is punishing. I am not so naive as to think that the road ahead will be without hardship or that the challenges to our sanity will not be vicious. My commitment is to make sure that this film is not buried or sidelined. And this commitment is uncompromising. I do not wish to be, as James Baldwin put it, an "eccentric patriot" or a "raving maniac."

THERE ARE NEW METAPHORS
MEETING GLORIA (BALDWIN KAREFA-SMART)

Wherefore Art Thou, Raoul? Wherever, pray All's Well. Don't know if you came across this JB quote, 1973: "There are new metaphors. There are new sounds. There are new relations. Men and Women will be different. Children will be different. They will have to make money obsolete. Make a man's life worth more than that. Restore the idea of work as joy, not drudgery."

—GLORIA KAREFA-SMART,
letter to Raoul Peck, April 2009

I first met James Baldwin's younger sister Gloria Karefa-Smart ten years ago, when she opened her door to me in a gentrified old black neighborhood of Washington, D.C., where she has lived since the days when it was a dangerous place to visit. I had written to the Baldwin estate two weeks earlier to ask for access to the biographical rights to James Baldwin's life and work; more vaguely, I especially wanted to ask for permission to work on a yet-to-be-defined film. What material to request exactly I was still unsure of at this stage. I didn't yet know what this arduous, impossible, unprecedented film project should or would be. I only knew that if I were going to tackle anything "Baldwin," it had better be strong and original.

And there I was, sipping tea with a soft-spoken, affable, and wise lady who had welcomed me into her refuge, which was rarely open to strangers. That day spent in Washington, D.C., was inspirational and most incredible. In Gloria, I had found a soul mate, a friend, and above all an ally with whom the conversation quickly became real, direct, sincere. I felt at home and welcomed.

Gloria had seen my films and in particular *Lumumba*, about the assassination of the first prime minister of Congo in 1961. She knew of my work and the themes I tackled. These subjects, I discovered, were also relevant in her own life and her own political narrative. Later this common interest transformed itself into indelible affection. Gloria was decisive in transforming my years of doubt, failure, and setbacks into wonderful years of passion and exhilarating discovery.

Since that first meeting, Gloria has never once left my life. She has always been there, accompanying me, supportive of the project, in times of trouble and lately in times of success. Her presence has been the most precious and cherished treasure of this entire journey.

The option granted to me by the estate was generous and unprecedented. As the years passed, unconcerned with the details of renewing the option, she allowed me to focus strictly on the success of the project and nothing else—which is an absolute exception in the business of film.

After four years of uncertain attempts on my part, Gloria one day gave me the decisive key to the film. She handed me a packet of some thirty pages of letters called "Notes Toward Remember This House," a book project that James Baldwin had never finished.

She casually told me, "Here Raoul, you'll know what to do with these."

And indeed, I knew immediately. A book that was never written! That's the story. And what characters! Medgar Evers, Malcolm X, and Martin Luther King, Jr. The notes themselves were not much to start with, but they were more than enough, given that I also had access to everything else from Baldwin. My job was to find that unwritten book. *I Am Not Your Negro* is the improbable result of that search.

So again, thank you, Gloria. Without your infinite patience, your discreet intelligence, and your limitless loving support, none of this would have become a reality.

NOTES ON
THE WRITING PROCESS

In all modesty, I profess I do not know of any other example of a film created strictly from the preexisting texts of one author. Especially when the texts came from sources as diverse as personal notes not intended for publication, letters, manuscripts, speeches, and published books. To begin with, I was theorizing, without any clearly defined guideline, about an inconceivable film.

So how to start concretely, practically?

After some blind wandering, I realized that without creating a first draft of a complete document, I would not be able to advance the realization of the film. But how to create such a text? It could not be an adaptation, or a simple compilation, let alone a chronological narration. I needed a dramatic structure, a story with a beginning, a middle, and an end, as I would for any screenplay. Except that in this particular case the words already existed, as if in a large jar filled with unlabeled pieces of a precious mosaic. Each piece, a promising diamond. A diamond that must be set to reveal its unique value, positioned for proper resonance, to create layered meanings and stories that interweave, contradict, and even collide with one another. I wanted to make, as Baldwin wrote in his notes, "a funky dish of chitterlings."

Like a librettist crafting the script for an opera from the scattered works of a revered author, I began my own journey, respecting at all times and preserving scrupulously the spirit, the philosophy, the pugnacity, the insight, the humor, the poetry, and the soul of the long-gone author.

It was clear from the start that countless traps lay ahead.

First, the material itself: several pages of notes typed, in no particular format, containing erasures, the object of repeated corrections. Even if it was evident from the outset that "Notes Toward Remember This House" was to be the foundation of this libretto, it was going to be hard work to find and include the additional texts that I needed to complete the manuscript and to do this without betraying or second-guessing Baldwin's thoughts or intentions.

The first draft was more than fifty pages long (three hours of film), a solid script that could become a coherent story. That was certainly reassuring, but it was just the beginning. From version to version, I allowed myself more freedom, reversing paragraphs, phrases, or, more rarely, words. Then I discovered advantageously that Baldwin often rewrote several times, in different documents, letters, or notes, the same sentence, idea, or narrative, with slight modifications or different argumentations. This meant that in some instances I was able to use the version that best suited the purpose, alter complicated digressions, or even mix the beginning of one version with the end of another. I hope that Mr. Baldwin will forgive this posthumous invasion of a writer's "kitchen."

Working on this manuscript provided me with a precious glimpse of a master at work, a chance to observe and understand how Baldwin crafted his writing, nurtured his thoughts. In places I discovered different articulations, in similar but staggered versions, of an idea or a reflection that would later in a separate composition take on a more definitive form. An observation made in a private letter to his brother David Baldwin could be sprinkled later in some notes and then end up as a scathing sentence in a published essay. Like many writers, Baldwin recycled notes and ideas several times before finding their final shape and destination. It was the juxtaposition of different versions that sometimes allowed me to find the necessary transitions or formulations for the elaboration of this manuscript.

Of course, there have been some infringements on the principle of remaining faithful to Baldwin's words. For example, where Baldwin wrote about "Bill," I chose to add the last name "Miller" for clarity. I silently corrected him when Baldwin erroneously referred to the actor Clinton Rosemond as "Clinton Rosewood" or mistyped Mantan Moreland's name as "Manton Moreand." Or again, when he wrote "Malcolm's oldest daughter, whose name is Stillah (I'm not sure of the spelling)," I corrected that to "Malcolm's oldest daughter, whose name is Attallah." In spite of these few exceptions, we remained to the end devoted to James Baldwin's thought, style, and choices.

What else is there to say? I hope not to have betrayed a man who has accompanied me from very early on, every day of my life, as a brother, father, mentor, accomplice, consoler, comrade-in-arms—an eternal witness of my own wanderings.

Thank you, my friend (if I may). You are forever inscribed in our memories and in our lives.

EDITING *I AM NOT YOUR NEGRO*
BY ALEXANDRA STRAUSS

Trying to make a film strictly from the point of view of a writer's mind is a major challenge—especially when the mind in question is so powerful, so articulate, and so magnificent and offers a vision that is profoundly humanistic, political, and philosophical. A film is a complex composition of sounds, music, and images deployed through many layers of editing. How can one translate written words into this form in a way that remains coherent and comprehensible? While reading a book, you can pause to take a second look. While watching a film, you can't. The perception of time is different, and the juxtaposition of images, sounds, and concepts has to be clear in the first viewing.

In *I Am Not Your Negro*, Raoul Peck wanted to bring into today's context the brilliant thinking of James Baldwin, an author he admires and whose work has engaged him for decades. Raoul's first compilation of all the materials and pieces of Baldwin's works he intended to use was massive. I was alarmed by the thought that we were heading toward creating a four-hour film. Even so, within this tentative and copious document, we could already clearly sense the general outline of meaningful images, chapters, and sequences. As a filmmaker, Raoul is adept with words and images, but the task of finding the right images for the right text in the right chronology and structure was an extremely complex endeavor.

Luckily, Baldwin had written extensively about cinema and its role in shaping our culture and ideology. The films Baldwin saw—the films that shaped his own mythology, that framed his childhood and marked him, as they marked Raoul's childhood a few decades later—provided the best vehicle for our audiovisual interpretation of Baldwin's vision. Beyond this, the pages of an incomplete manuscript entitled *Remember This House*, given to Raoul by the Baldwin family, gave us the narrative direction for the film—a film that would be this unfinished book or at least a vivid projection of what that book might have encompassed.

Early on, we knew that this was going to be neither a film about civil rights nor a biographical film, without, however, completely avoiding either. The most delicate question was rather how to tie the heterogeneous material of Baldwin's unfinished project about his three friends—Martin Luther King, Jr., Medgar Evers, and Malcolm X—together with his words, his experience, his life, and his commitment to form a comprehensive and uncompromising monument to Baldwin.

The first edit was a test for us: How do we connect a narrating voice that obviously could not be Baldwin's with the real footage of him speaking so eloquently? How could we achieve a discursive continuity between these two elements? Further, how to find the appropriate images that would resonate with the written words?

Our archivist, Marie-Hélène Barbéris, faced a difficult and compelling task: researching, assembling, and cataloging hundreds of photos, old movies, newsreels, newspaper headlines, advertisements, and amateur videos, all in different formats and styles. We faced countless complications

in the variable quality of some of the material, in getting
access, and in clearing rights that were often spread among
multiple rights holders. The process presented at times an
improbable spiderweb of complexity.

But gradually the film found its form, its rhythm, and its
autonomy. We worked in complete freedom in terms of the
production process, iconographic choices, content, form,
and time, which is a luxury these days. During the two full
years that I worked on the film, I was able to take time off,
either to work on other projects or to get some valuable dis-
tance from the current edit and come back with fresh ideas,
new resolutions, and creative solutions. Meanwhile, Marie-
Hélène and her team continually deepened their research
and supplied us with new and rare material. Our freedom
also depended on the producer's ability to find additional
funding, allowing us to extend our scope. This generous production framework was key to our creativity and efficiency.

Raoul Peck trusted me to bring to his film my own sen-
sibility, my ideas, and something else I find essential, which
is hard to describe but that I would call a kind of poetic,
intuitive inspiration.

Jean-Luc Godard wrote, "If directing is a vision, *editing*
is the *heartbeat*." His words describe the very core of cinema
and its mystery. This was our guiding assumption during
the improbable journey of this film as we worked to bring
the past into the present moment through James Baldwin's
finest writing.

I AM NOT
YOUR NEGRO

In June 1979,
acclaimed author James Baldwin
commits to a complex endeavor:

tell his story of America
through the lives of three
of his murdered friends:

Medgar Evers
Martin Luther King, Jr.
Malcolm X

Baldwin never got past
his thirty pages of notes,
entitled: *Remember This House*

THE DICK CAVETT SHOW - 1968 -

DICK CAVETT: *Mr. Baldwin, I'm sure you still meet the remark: "What are the Negroes . . . why aren't they optimistic?"*

But they say it's getting so much better. There are Negro mayors. There are Negroes in all of sports. There are Negroes in politics. They are even accorded the ultimate accolade of being in television commercials now. I'm glad you're smiling. Is it at once getting much better and still hopeless?

JAMES BALDWIN: *Well, I don't think there's much hope for it, you know, to tell you the truth as long as people are using this peculiar language. It's not a question of what happens to the Negro here or to the black man here—that's a very vivid question for me, you know—but the real question is what is going to happen to this country. I have to repeat that.*

To Jay Acton
Spartan Literary Agency

June 30th, 1979

My dear Jay,

I'll confess to you that I am writing the
enclosed proposal in a somewhat divided
frame of mind. The summer has scarcely
begun, and I feel, already, that it's
almost over.

And I will be fifty-five (yes! fifty-
five!) in a month. I am about to
undertake the journey: and this is a
journey, to tell you the truth, which I
always knew that I would have to make,
but had hoped, perhaps (certainly, I had
hoped), not to have to make so soon.

I am saying that a journey is called
that because you cannot know what you
will discover on the journey, what you
will do with what you find, or what you
find will do to you.

MARTIN LUTHER KING: *Not only do we have the right to be free,*
we have a duty to be free. So when you sit down on a bus,
when you sit down in the front, or you sit down by a white
person, you are sitting down because you have a duty to sit
down not merely because you have a right.

The time of these lives and deaths,
from a public point of view,
is 1955, when we first heard of Martin,
to 1968, when he was murdered.
Medgar was murdered in the summer of 1963.
Malcolm was murdered in 1965.

The three men—
Medgar, Malcolm, and Martin—
were very different men.
Consider that Martin was only twenty-six in 1955.
He took on his shoulders the weight of the crimes,
and the lies and the hope of a nation.

I want these three lives to bang against
and reveal each other,
as, in truth, they did . . .
and use their dreadful journey
as a means of instructing the people
whom they loved so much,
who betrayed them,
and for whom they gave their lives.

PAYING MY DUES

LEANDER PEREZ, WHITE CITIZENS COUNCIL: *The moment a Negro child walks into the school, every decent, self-respecting, loving parent should take his white child out of that broken school.*

WOMAN IN THE SOUTH: *God forgives murder and he forgives adultery. But he is very angry and he actually curses all who do integrate.*

That's when I saw the photograph.
Facing us, on every newspaper kiosk
on that wide, tree-shaded boulevard in Paris
were photographs of fifteen-year-old Dorothy Counts
being reviled and spat upon by the mob
as she was making her way to school
in Charlotte, North Carolina.

There was unutterable pride, tension, and anguish
in that girl's face
as she approached the halls of learning,
with history, jeering, at her back.

It made me furious,
it filled me with both hatred and pity.
And it made me ashamed.

Some one of us should have been there with her!

But it was on that bright afternoon
that I knew I was leaving France.
I could, simply, no longer sit around
in Paris discussing the Algerian
and the black American problem.
Everybody else was paying their dues,
and it was time I went home and paid mine.

I had at last come home.
If there was, in this, some illusion,
there was also much truth.

In the years in Paris,
I had never been homesick for anything American—
neither waffles, ice cream, hot dogs,
baseball, majorettes, movies,
nor the Empire State Building, nor Coney Island,
nor the Statue of Liberty, nor the *Daily News*,
nor Times Square.
All of these things had passed out of me.
They might never have existed,
and it made absolutely no difference to me
if I never saw them again.

But I had missed my brothers and sisters,
and my mother.
They made a difference.
I wanted to be able to see them,
and to see their children.
I hoped that they wouldn't forget me.

———————

I missed Harlem Sunday mornings
and fried chicken and biscuits,
I missed the music,
I missed the style—
that style possessed by no other people in the world.
I missed the way the dark face closes,
the way dark eyes watch,
and the way, when a dark face opens,
a light seems to go everywhere.
I missed, in short, my connections,
missed the life which had produced me
and nourished me and paid for me.
Now, though I was a stranger,
I was home.

I am fascinated by the movement
on and off the screen.
I am about seven.
I am with my mother, or my aunt.
The movie is *Dance, Fools, Dance.*
I was aware that Joan Crawford was a white lady.
Yet, I remember being sent
to the store sometime later,
and a colored woman, who, to me, looked exactly
like Joan Crawford, was buying something.
She was incredibly beautiful. . . .
She looked down at me with so beautiful a smile that
I was not even embarrassed.
Which was rare for me.

HEROES

By this time,
I had been taken in hand by a young white
schoolteacher named Bill Miller,
a beautiful woman,
very important to me.
She gave me books to read and talked to me
about the books,
and about the world:
about Ethiopia,
and Italy,
and the German Third Reich;
and took me to see plays and films, to which no one
else would have dreamed of taking a ten-year-old boy.

It is certainly because of Bill Miller,
who arrived in my terrifying life so soon,
that I never really managed to hate white people.
Though, God knows,
I have often wished to murder more than one or two.

Therefore, I begin to suspect that white people
did not act as they did because they were white,
but for some other reason.

I was a child of course,
and, therefore, unsophisticated.
I took Bill Miller as she was,
or as she appeared to be to me.
She too, anyway, was treated like a nigger,

especially by the cops.
And she had no love for landlords.

In these days, no one resembling my father has yet
made an appearance on the American cinema scene.
No, it is not entirely true.
There were, for example, Stepin Fetchit
and Willie Best and Mantan Moreland,
all of whom, rightly or wrongly, I loathed.
It seemed to me that they lied about the world
I knew, and debased it,
and certainly I did not know anybody like them—
as far as I could tell;
for it is also possible that their comic, bug-eyed terror
contained the truth concerning a terror
by which I hoped never to be engulfed.

Yet, I had no reservations at all concerning the terror
of the black janitor in *They Won't Forget*.
I think that it was a black actor named
Clinton Rosemond who played this part,
and he looked a little like my father.
He is terrified because a young white girl,
in this small Southern town, has been raped
and murdered, and her body has been found
on the premises of which he is the janitor.

————

The role of the janitor is small,
yet the man's face bangs in my memory until today:
the film's icy brutality both
scared me and strengthened me.

Because Uncle Tom refuses to take vengeance
in his own hands, he was not a hero for me.
Heroes, as far as I could see, were white,
and not merely because of the movies
but because of the land in which I lived,
of which movies were simply a reflection.

I despised and feared those heroes because
they did take vengeance into their own hands.
They thought vengeance was theirs to take.
And yes. I understood that:
my countrymen were my enemy.

I suspect that all these stories are designed
to reassure us that no crime was committed.
We've made a legend out of a massacre.

JAMES BALDWIN AND
WILLIAM F. BUCKLEY, JR.,
CAMBRIDGE UNIVERSITY DEBATE - 1965 -

JAMES BALDWIN: *Leaving aside all the physical facts which one can quote, leaving aside rape or murder, leaving aside the bloody catalogue of oppression, which we are in one way too familiar with already, what this does to the subjugated—is to destroy his sense of reality.*

This means in the case of the American Negro, born in that glittering republic . . . and in the moment you are born, since you don't know any better, every stick and stone and every face is white, and since you have not yet seen a mirror, you suppose that you are, too. It comes as a great shock around the age of five, or six, or seven to discover that Gary Cooper killing off the Indians when you were rooting for Gary Cooper, that the Indians were you.

It comes as a great shock to discover the country which is your birthplace and to which you owe your life and your identity has not in its whole system of reality evolved any place for you.

My dear Jay,

You must, it is to be hoped, be as
curious as I am concerning the execution
of this book project.

I know how to do it, technically.
It is a matter of research, and journeys.
And, with you, or without you, I will do
it anyway.

I begin in September, when I go on the
road. "The road" means my return to the
South. It means, briefly, for example,
seeing Myrlie Evers, and the children—
those children, who are children no
longer. It means going back to Atlanta,
to Selma, to Birmingham. It means
seeing Coretta Scott King, and Martin's
children.

I know that Martin's daughter, whose
name I don't remember, and Malcolm's
oldest daughter, whose name is Attallah,
are both in the theater, and apparently,
are friends.

It means seeing Betty Shabazz, Malcolm's
widow, and the five younger children.
It means exposing myself as one of
the witnesses to the lives and deaths
of their famous fathers. And it means
much, much more than that—a cloud of
witnesses, as old St. Paul once put it.

WITNESS

I first met Malcolm X.
I saw Malcolm before I met him.
I was giving a lecture somewhere in New York.
Malcolm was sitting in the first row of the hall,
bending forward at such an angle
that his long arms nearly caressed the ankles
of his long legs, staring up at me.
I very nearly panicked.
I knew Malcolm only by legend,
and this legend, since I was a Harlem street boy,
I was sufficiently astute to distrust.

Malcolm might be the torch
that white people claim he was—
though, in general, white America's evaluations
of these matters would be laughable
and even pathetic did not these evaluations
have such wicked results.
On the other hand, Malcolm had
no reason to trust me, either.
And so I stumbled through my lecture,
with Malcolm never taking his eyes from my face.

As a member of the NAACP,
Medgar was investigating the murder
of a black man, which had occurred months before;
had shown me letters from black people,
asking him to do this;
and he had asked me to come with him.

I was terribly frightened,
but perhaps that "field trip" will help us define
what I mean by the word "witness."

I was to discover that the line which separates
a witness from an actor is a very thin line indeed;
nevertheless, the line is real.

I was not, for example, a Black Muslim,
in the same way, though for different reasons,
that I never became a Black Panther:
because I did not believe that
all white people were devils,
and I did not want
young black people to believe that.
I was not a member of any Christian congregation
because I knew that they had not heard
and did not live by the commandment
"love one another as I love you,"
and I was not a member of the NAACP
because in the North, where I grew up,
the NAACP was fatally entangled
with black class distinctions,
or illusions of the same,
which repelled a shoe-shine boy like me.

I did not have to deal with
the criminal state of Mississippi,
hour by hour and day by day,
to say nothing of night after night.
I did not have to sweat cold sweat after decisions
involving hundreds of thousands of lives.

I was not responsible for raising money,
for deciding how to use it.
I was not responsible for strategy controlling
prayer meetings, marches, petitions,
voting registration drives.
I saw the sheriffs, the deputies, the storm troopers
more or less in passing.
I was never in town to stay.
This was sometimes hard on my morale,
but I had to accept, as time wore on,
that part of my responsibility—as a witness—
was to move as largely and as freely as possible,
to write the story, and to get it out.

FBI REPORT
March, 1966
FBI MEMORANDUM

Information concerning
James Arthur Baldwin

To assistant FBI director Alan Rosen

Bureau files reveal that Baldwin, a
negro author, was born in NYC and
has lived and travelled in Europe.
He has become rather well-known
due to his writing dealing with the
relationship of whites and negroes.
It has been heard that Baldwin may
be an homosexual and he appeared as
if he may be one.

J. EDGAR HOOVER: *We should all be concerned with but one goal: the eradication of crime. The Federal Bureau of Investigation is as close to you as your nearest telephone. It seeks to be your protector in all matters within its jurisdiction. It belongs to you.*

FBI REPORT

Information collected clearly
depicted the subject as a
dangerous individual who could be
expected to commit acts
inimical to the national defense
and public safety to the United
States in times of emergency.
Consequently his name is being
included in the security index.

White people are astounded by Birmingham.
Black people aren't.
White people are endlessly demanding to be
reassured that Birmingham is really on Mars.
They don't want to believe,
still less to act on the belief,
that what is happening in Birmingham
is happening all over the country.
They don't want to realize that there is not one step,
morally or actually, between
Birmingham and Los Angeles.

THE NEGRO AND THE AMERICAN PROMISE - 1963 -

DR. KENNETH CLARK: *We've invited three men on the forefront of the Negro struggle to sit down and talk with us in front of the television camera. Each of these men through his actions and his words, but with vastly different manner and means, is a spokesman for some segment of the Negro people today.*

MALCOLM X: *Black people in this country have been the victims of violence at the hands of the white man for four hundred years. And following the ignorant Negro preachers, we have thought that it was godlike to turn the other cheek to the brute that was brutalizing us.*

KENNETH CLARK: *Malcolm X, one of the most articulate exponents of the Black Muslim philosophy, has said of your movement and your philosophy that it plays into the hands of the white oppressor, that they are happy to hear you talk about love for the oppressor because this disarms the Negro and fits into the stereotype of the Negro as a meek, turning-the-other-cheek sort of creature. Would you care to comment on Mr. X's beliefs?*

MARTIN LUTHER KING: *Well, I don't think of love as, in this context, as emotional bosh, but I think of love as something strong and that organizes itself into powerful direct action. This is what I have tried to teach in the struggle in the South, that we are not engaged in a struggle that means we sit down and do nothing. There is a great deal of difference between nonresistance to evil and nonviolent resistance.*

MALCOLM X: *Martin Luther King is just a twentieth-century or a modern Uncle Tom, or a religious Uncle Tom, who is doing the same thing today to keep Negroes defenseless in the face of attack that Uncle Tom did on the plantation to keep those Negroes defenseless in the face of the attacks of the Klan in that day.*

MARTIN LUTHER KING: *I think though that we can be sure that the vast majority of Negroes who engage in the demonstrations and who understand the nonviolent philosophy will be able to face dogs and all of the other brutal methods that are used without retaliating with violence, because they understand that one of the first principles of nonviolence is a willingness to be the recipient of violence, while never inflicting violence on another.*

As concerns Malcolm and Martin,
I watched two men, coming from
unimaginably different backgrounds,
whose positions, originally, were poles apart,
driven closer and closer together.

By the time each died, their positions
had become virtually the same position.
It can be said, indeed, that Martin
picked up Malcolm's burden,
articulated the vision which
Malcolm had begun to see,
and for which he paid with his life.
And that Malcolm was one of the people
Martin saw on the mountaintop.

Medgar was too young to have seen this happen,
though he hoped for it,
and would not have been surprised;
but Medgar was murdered first.

I was older than Medgar, Malcolm, and Martin.
I was raised to believe that the eldest
was supposed to be a model for the younger,
and was, of course, expected to die first.

Not one of these three lived to be forty.

MALCOLM X: *We need an organization that no one downtown loves. We need one that is ready and willing to take action, any kind of action by any means necessary.*

JAMES BALDWIN: *When Malcolm talks, or the other Muslim ministers talk, they articulate for all the Negro people who hear them, who listen to them, they articulate their suffering. The suffering which has been in this country so long denied. That is Malcolm's great authority over any of his audiences. He corroborates their reality. He tells them that they really exist, you know.*

There are days—this is one of them—when you wonder what your role is in this country and what your future is in it. How precisely are you going to reconcile yourself to your situation here and how you are going to communicate to the vast, heedless, unthinking, cruel white majority that you are here. I'm terrified at the moral apathy, the death of the heart, which is happening in my country. These people have deluded themselves for so long that they really don't think I'm human. And I base this on their conduct, not on what they say. And this means that they have become in themselves moral monsters.

FLORIDA FORUM - 1963 -

JAMES BALDWIN: *Most of the white Americans I've ever encountered, really, you know, had a Negro friend or a Negro maid or somebody in high school, but they never, you know, or rarely, after school was over or whatever came to my kitchen, you know. We were segregated from the schoolhouse door. Therefore, he doesn't know, he really does not know, what it was like for me to leave my house, you know, to leave the school and go back to Harlem. He doesn't know how Negroes live. And it comes as a great surprise to the Kennedy brothers and to everybody else in the country. I'm certain, again, you know . . . that again like most white Americans I have encountered, they have no . . . I'm sure they have nothing whatever against Negroes, but that's really not the question, you know. The question is really a kind of apathy and ignorance, which is the price we pay for segregation. That's what segregation means. You don't know what's happening on the other side of the wall, because you don't want to know.*

I was, in some way, in those years,
without entirely realizing it,
the Great Black Hope of the Great White Father.
I was *not* a racist—
or so I thought;
Malcolm *was* a racist,
or so *they* thought.

In fact, we were simply trapped in the same situation.

A RAISIN IN THE SUN

SIDNEY POITIER: *Well you tell that to my boy tonight, when you put him to sleep on the living room couch. You tell it to him in the morning when his mother goes out of here to take care of somebody else's kids. And tell it to me, when we want some curtains or some drapes and you sneak out of here and go work in somebody's kitchen. All I want is to make a future for this family. All I want is to be able to stand in front of my boy like my father never was able to do to me.*

I must sketch now
the famous Bobby Kennedy meeting.

Lorraine Hansberry would not be very much
younger than I am now if she were alive.
At the time of the Bobby Kennedy meeting,
she was thirty-three.
That was one of the very last times
I saw her on her feet,
and she died at the age of thirty-four.

I miss her so much.

People forget how young everybody was.
Bobby Kennedy, for another, quite different,
example, was thirty-eight.

We wanted him to tell his brother the President
to personally escort to school,
on that day or the day after,
a small black girl already scheduled
to enter a Deep South school.
"That way," we said,
"it will be clear that whoever spits on that child
will be spitting on the nation."
He didn't understand this either.
"It would be," he said, "a meaningless moral gesture."

"We would like," said Lorraine,
"from you, a moral commitment."

He looked insulted—seemed to feel
that he had been wasting his time.
Well Lorraine sat still, watching all the while . . .
She looked at Bobby Kennedy, who,
perhaps for the first time, looked at her.
"But I am very worried," she said,
"about the state of the civilization which produced
that photograph of the white cop standing
on that Negro woman's neck in Birmingham."

Then, she smiled.
And I am glad that she was not smiling at me.
"Goodbye, Mr. Attorney General," she said,
and turned and walked out of the room.

And then, we heard the thunder.

The very last time I saw Medgar Evers,
he stopped at his house on the way to the airport
so I could autograph my books for him,
his wife and children.
I remember Myrlie Evers standing outside, smiling,
and we waved,
and Medgar drove to the airport
and put me on the plane.

Months later,
I was in Puerto Rico, working on my play.
Lucien and I had spent a day or so
wandering around the island,
and now we were driving home.
It was a wonderful, bright, sunny day,
the top to the car was down,
we were laughing and talking,
and the radio was playing.
Then the music stopped . . .

. . . and a voice announced that Medgar Evers
had been shot to death in the carport of his home,
and his wife and children had seen the big man fall.

"ONLY A PAWN IN THEIR GAME," BOB DYLAN

Today, Medgar Evers was buried from the bullet he caught.
They lowered him down as a king.
But when the shadowy sun sets on the one
That fired the gun
He'll see by his grave
On the stone that remains
Carved next to his name
His epitaph plain:
Only a pawn in their game.

The blue sky seemed to descend like a blanket.
And I couldn't say anything,
I couldn't cry;
I just remembered his face,
a bright, blunt, handsome face,
and his weariness, which he wore like his skin,
and the way he said *ro-aad* for road,
and his telling me how the tatters of clothes
from a lynched body hung,
flapping, in the tree for days,
and how he had to pass that tree every day.

Medgar.
Gone.

In America, I was free only in battle,
never free to rest—
and he who finds no way to rest
cannot long survive the battle. . . .
And a young, white revolutionary remains,
in general, far more romantic
than a black one.

White people have managed to get through
entire lifetimes in this euphoric state,
but black people have not been so lucky:
a black man who sees the world the way
John Wayne, for example, sees it

would not be an eccentric patriot,
but a raving maniac.

The truth is that this country does not know
what to do with its black population,
dreaming of anything like "the final solution."

THE NEGRO AND THE AMERICAN PROMISE - 1963 -

JAMES BALDWIN: *The Negro has never been as docile as white Americans wanted to believe. That was a myth. We were not singing and dancing down on the levee. We were trying to keep alive; we were trying to survive a very brutal system. The "nigger" has never been happy in his place.*

BALDWIN'S NIGGER - 1969 -

JAMES BALDWIN: *One of the most terrible things is that in fact, whether I like it or not, I am an American. My school really was the streets of New York City. My frame of reference was George Washington and John Wayne. But, I was a child, you know, and when a child puts his eyes in the world he has to use what he sees. There's nothing else to use. And you are formed by what you see, the choices you have to make, and the way you discover what it means to be black in New York and then throughout the entire country.*

I know how you watch as you grow older, and it is not a figure of speech, the corpses of your brothers and your sisters pile up around you. And not for anything they have done. They were too young to have done anything. But what one does realize is that when you try to stand up and look the world in the face like you had a right to be here, you have attacked the entire power structure of the Western world.

*Forget the Negro problem. Don't write any voting acts.
We had that—it's called the fifteenth amendment—during
the Civil Rights Bill of 1964. What you have to look at
is what is happening in this country, and what is really
happening is that brother has murdered brother knowing it
was his brother. White men have lynched Negroes knowing
them to be their sons. White women have had Negroes
burned knowing them to be their lovers. It is not a racial
problem. It is a problem of whether or not you're willing to
look at your life and be responsible for it, and then begin
to change it. That great Western house I come from is one
house, and I am one of the children of that house. Simply, I
am the most despised child of that house. And it is because
the American people are unable to face the fact that I am
flesh of their flesh, bone of their bone, created by them. My
blood, my father's blood, is in that soil.*

IMITATION OF LIFE - 1934 -

MOTHER: *Good afternoon, ma'am. It's raining so hard, I
brought rubbers and a coat to fetch my little girl home.*
TEACHER: *I'm afraid you've made some mistake.*
MOTHER: *Ain't this 3B?*
TEACHER: *Yes.*
MOTHER: *Well this is it.*

TEACHER: *She can't be. I have no little colored children in my class.*

MOTHER: *Oh. Thank you. . . . There's my little girl.*

TEACHER: *Peola, you may go home.*

CLASSMATE #1: *Gee, I didn't know she was colored.*

CLASSMATE #2: *Neither did I.*

PEOLA: *I hate you, I hate you, I hate you!*

MOTHER: *Peola! Peola!*

PURITY

I know very well that my ancestors
had no desire to come to this place.
But neither did the ancestors of the people
who became white and who require
of my captivity a song.
They require a song of me
less to celebrate my captivity
than to justify their own.

———

I have always been struck, in America,
by an emotional poverty so bottomless,
and a terror of human life, of human touch, so deep,
that virtually no American appears able to achieve
any viable, organic connection
between his public stance and his private life.
This failure of the private life
has always had the most devastating effect
on American public conduct,
and on black-white relations.
If Americans were not so terrified
of their private selves,
they would never have become so dependent
on what they call "the Negro problem."

NO WAY OUT - 1950 -

RICHARD WIDMARK: *They said it wasn't nice to say nigger. Nigger! Nigger! Nigger! Poor little nigger kids, love the little nigger kids. Who loved me? Who loved me?*

This problem, which they invented
in order to safeguard their purity,
has made of them criminals and monsters,
and it is destroying them.

And this, not from anything blacks
may or may not be doing
but because of the role of a guilty
and constricted white imagination
as assigned to the blacks.

THE DEFIANT ONES - 1958 -

TONY CURTIS: *Look, man, don't give me that look. You should have got what was coming to you after spitting in that guy's face. . . . (Sidney slaps the cigarette from Tony Curtis's mouth.) Why you . . . (The two men fight.)*

SIDNEY POITIER: *That time is now.*

SIDNEY POITIER: *Run! Come on!*

TONY CURTIS: *I can't make it, I can't make it!*

It is impossible to accept the premise of the story,
a premise based on the profound
American misunderstanding
of the nature of the hatred between black and white.
The root of the black man's hatred is rage,
and he does not so much hate white men
as simply wants them out of his way,
and, more than that,
out of his children's way.

The root of the white man's hatred is terror,
a bottomless and nameless terror,
which focuses on this dread figure,
an entity which lives only in his mind.

When Sidney jumps off the train,
the white liberal people downtown
were much relieved and joyful.
But when black people saw him jump off the train,
they yelled, "Get back on the train, you fool."

The black man jumps off the train
in order to reassure white people,
to make them know that they are not hated;
that, though they have made human errors,
they've done nothing for which to be hated.

CHIQUITA BANANA ADVERTISEMENT

I'm Chiquita Banana, and I'm here to say
I am the top banana . . .

In spite of the fabulous myths proliferating in this
country concerning the sexuality of black people,
black men are still used,
in the popular culture,
as though they had no sexual equipment at all.

Sidney Poitier,
as a black artist, and a man, is also up against
the infantile, furtive sexuality of this country.
Both he and Harry Belafonte, for example,
are sex symbols, though no one dares admit that,
still less to use them as any of
the Hollywood he-men are used.

Black people have been robbed
of everything in this country,
and they don't want to be robbed of their artists.

Black people particularly disliked
Guess Who's Coming to Dinner
because they felt that Sidney was,
in effect, being used against them.

Guess Who's Coming to Dinner may prove,
in some bizarre way, to be a milestone,
because it is really quite impossible to go
any further in that particular direction.
The next time,
the kissing will have to start.

IN THE HEAT OF THE NIGHT - 1967 -

ROD STEIGER: *Well, you've got your ticket? Here you are.*
Thank you. . . .
ROD STEIGER: *Virgil! You take care, you hear?*
SIDNEY POITIER: *Yeah.*

I am aware that men do not kiss
each other in American films,
nor for the most part, in America, nor do the black
detective and the white sheriff kiss here.
But the obligatory fade-out kiss,
in the classic American film,
did not speak of love, and, still less, of sex:
it spoke of reconciliation,
of all things now becoming possible.

I knew a blond girl in the Village a long time ago,
and, eventually, we never walked
out of the house together.
She was far safer walking the streets alone
than when walking with me—
a brutal and humiliating fact which thoroughly
destroyed whatever relationship this girl and
I might have been able to achieve.
This happens all the time in America,
but Americans have yet to realize what a sinister fact
this is, and what it says about them.
When we walked out in the evening, then,
she would leave ahead of me, alone.
I would give her about five minutes,
and then I would walk out alone, taking another
route, and meet her on the subway platform.
We would not acknowledge each other.
We would get into the subway car,
sitting at opposite ends of it,
and walk, separately, through the streets
of the free and the brave,
to wherever we were going—
a friend's house, or the movies.

THE SECRET OF SELLING THE NEGRO

THE SECRET OF SELLING THE NEGRO - 1954 -

All over the country, families such as this one are enjoying new prosperity. They have new interests, new standards of living, a buying power they've never enjoyed before. They are good prospects for practically all types of goods and services. All too often, though, they are overlooked prospects. Since 1940 in San Francisco alone, the Negro market has increased by 89 percent. Here are millions of customers for what you have to sell. Customers with 15 billion dollars to spend.

Someone once said to me that the people in general
cannot bear very much reality.
He meant by this that they prefer fantasy
to a truthful re-creation of their experience.

The people have quite enough reality to bear
by simply getting through their lives,
raising their children,
dealing with the eternal conundrums
of birth, taxes, and death.

ROBERT KENNEDY: *Negroes are continuously making progress here in this country. The progress in many areas is not as fast as it should be, but they are making progress, and we will continue to make progress. There is no reason that in the near and the foreseeable future that a Negro could not also be president of the United States.*

CAMBRIDGE UNIVERSITY DEBATE - 1965 -

JAMES BALDWIN: *I remember, for example, when the ex–Attorney General, Mr. Robert Kennedy, said that it was conceivable that in forty years in America we might have a Negro president. And that sounded like a very emancipated statement, I suppose, to white people. They were not in Harlem when this statement was first heard. They did not hear (and possibly will never hear) the laughter and the*

bitterness and the scorn with which this statement was greeted. From the point of view of the man in the Harlem barbershop, Bobby Kennedy only got here yesterday and now he's already on his way to the presidency. We've been here for four hundred years and now he tells us that maybe in forty years, if you're good, we may let you become president.

SELLING THE NEGRO

JAMES BALDWIN: *Let me put it this way: that from a very literal point of view, the harbors and the ports and the railroads of the country; the economy, especially of the Southern states, could not conceivably be what it has become if they had not had, and do not still have, indeed, and for so long—so many generations—cheap labor.*

It is a terrible thing for an entire people to surrender to the notion that one-ninth of its population is beneath them. And until that moment, until the moment comes when we the Americans, we the American people, are able to accept the fact that I have to accept, for example, that my ancestors are both white and black, that on that continent we are trying to forge a new identity for which we need each other, and that I am not a ward of America, I am not an object of missionary charity, I am one of the people who built the country. Until this moment, there is scarcely any hope for the American dream, because people who are denied participation in it, by their very presence, will wreck it. And if that happens, it is a very grave moment for the West. Thank you.

HOLLYWOOD ROUNDTABLE - 1963 -

DAVID SCHOENBURN: *We're here in the studio today with seven men who have two things in common: they are entertainers and artists; and they've all come to Washington. They are seven out of some two hundred thousand American citizens who came to the capital to march for freedom and for jobs. Will this tremendous outburst now lead to a course of action, Mr. Belafonte?*

HARRY BELAFONTE: *The now that is being spoken about is the fact that in a hundred years, finally, through whatever the causes have been in history—and most of them have been because of oppression—the Negro people have strongly and fully taken the bit in their teeth and are asking for absolutely no quarter from anyone. But I do say that the bulk of the interpretation of whether this thing is going to end successfully and joyously or is going to end disastrously lays very heavily with the white community, it lays very heavily with the profiteers, it lays very heavily with the vested interests, it lays very heavily with a great middle stream in this country of people who have refused to commit themselves or even have the slightest knowledge that these things have been going on.*

I am speaking as a member of a certain democracy
in a very complex country which insists
on being very narrow-minded.

Simplicity is taken to be a great American virtue
along with sincerity.

APOLOGY SEQUENCE

I'm sorry. [Richard Nixon]
I'm deeply sorry. [Larry Craig]
And I'm sorry. [Rahm Emanuel]
I'm deeply sorry about that. [Arnold Schwarzenegger]
There are no excuses. [John Rowland]
I am sorry . . . [Bill Clinton]
We have made plenty of mistakes. [Ronald Reagan]
For that I apologize. [Todd Akin]
I am very sorry. [Hillary Clinton]
I am sorry I did this to you, but you have to get used to it.
It's one of those little problems in life. [Donald Trump]
I take full responsibility. [John Ensign]
I am here today to again apologize. [Anthony Weiner]
I apologize for the fact . . . to her . . . [Robert Bentley]
For any mistakes I've made, I take full responsibility. It's an
honor to serve the city of Ferguson and the people who live
there. [Thomas Jackson]

One of the results of this is that
immaturity is taken to be a virtue, too.
So that someone like that, let's say John Wayne
who spent most of his time
on screen admonishing Indians,
was in no necessity to grow up.

I had been in London on this particular night.
We were free and we decided to treat ourselves
to a really fancy, friendly dinner.
The headwaiter came, and said
there was a phone call for me,
and my sister Gloria rose to take it.
She was very strange when she came back—
she didn't say anything,
and I began to be afraid to ask her anything.
Then, nibbling at something she obviously
wasn't tasting, she said,
"Well, I've got to tell you because the press is on its
way over here. They have just killed Malcolm."

THE DICK CAVETT SHOW - 1968 -

JAMES BALDWIN: *There is nothing in the evidence offered by the book of the American republic which allows me really to argue with the cat who says to me: "They needed us to pick the cotton and now they don't need us anymore. Now they don't need us, they're going to kill us all off. Just like they did the Indians." And I can't say it's a Christian nation, that your brothers will never do that to you, because the record is too long and too bloody. That's all we have done. All your buried corpses now begin to speak.*

H. RAP BROWN (1967): *I say violence is necessary, violence is a part of American culture. It is as American as cherry pie. Black power, brothers.*

THE DICK CAVETT SHOW - 1968 -

JAMES BALDWIN: *If we were white, if we were Irish, if we were Jewish, if we were Poles, if we had, in fact, in your mind a frame of reference our heroes would be your heroes, too. Nat Turner would be a hero for you instead of a threat. Malcolm X might still be alive. Everyone is very proud of brave little Israel—against which I have nothing; I don't want to be misinterpreted, I am not an anti-Semite. But, you know, when the Israelis pick up guns, or the Poles, or the Irish, or any white man in the world says "give me liberty, or give me death," the entire white world applauds. When a black man says exactly the same thing, word for word, he is judged a criminal and treated like one and everything*

*possible is done to make an example of this bad nigger, so
there won't be any more like him.*

THE LAND WE LOVE - U.S. GOVERNMENT FILM, 1960 -

*Look out across this land we love. Look about you,
wherever you are. There's unending scenic beauty and
there's freedom. It's an inherent American right meaning
many different things to every single citizen.*

*It's a leisurely afternoon of golf along a pleasant course.
It's an amusement park, a roller coaster ride. A day at the
county fair. A day of excitement, unrestricted travel across
all our fifty states, unlimited enjoyment of all these jewels
in the continent's crown. For all of us, there's all of America,
all of its scenic beauty, all of its heritage of history, all of its
limitless opportunity. . . .*

MARTIN LUTHER KING (speaking at a rally): *We've dropped too
many bombs on Vietnam now. Let us save our national
honor. Stop the bombing! And stop the war!*

What I'm trying to say to this country,
to us,
is that we must know this . . .

. . . we must realize this,
that no other country in the world has been
so fat and so sleek, and so safe, and so happy,
and so irresponsible, and so dead.
No other country can afford to dream of a Plymouth
and a wife and a house with a fence and the children
growing up safely to go to college and
to become executives, and then to marry and
have the Plymouth and the house and so forth.
A great many people do not live this way
and cannot imagine it, and do not know
that when we talk about "democracy,"
this is what we mean.

The industry is compelled, given the way
it is built, to present to the American people
a self-perpetuating fantasy of American life.

Their concept of entertainment is difficult
to distinguish from the use of narcotics.

THE TRISHA GODDARD SHOW

TRISHA GODDARD: *What worries you about [your daughters] having black partners? Do you think people are going to look down on them? Or judge them?*
MOTHER: *Yes, I think people look down on them.*

To watch the TV screen for any length of time
is to learn some really frightening things
about the American sense of reality.

We are cruelly trapped between
what we would like to be and what we actually are.
And we cannot possibly become
what we would like to be until we are willing
to ask ourselves just why the lives we lead
on this continent are mainly so empty, so tame,
and so ugly.

These images are designed not to trouble,
but to reassure.
They also weaken our ability to deal
with the world as it is, ourselves as we are.

THE DICK CAVETT SHOW - 1968 -

DICK CAVETT: *I would like to add someone to our group here, Professor Paul Weiss, the Sterling Professor of Philosophy at Yale. (Weiss enters.) Were you able to listen to the show backstage?*

PAUL WEISS: *I heard a good deal of it, but then I was behind the (inaudible), so I heard only some of it.*

DICK CAVETT: *Did you hear anything that you disagreed with?*

PAUL WEISS: *I disagreed with a great deal of it . . . of course, there's a good deal I agree with. But I think he's overlooking one very important matter, I think. Each one of us, I think, is terribly alone. He lives his own individual life. He has all kinds of obstacles in the way of religion or color or size or shape or lack of ability, and the problem is to become a man.*

JAMES BALDWIN: *But what I was discussing was not that problem, really. I was discussing the difficulties, the obstacles, the very real danger of death thrown up by the society when a Negro, when a black man attempts to become a man.*

PAUL WEISS: *All this emphasis upon black man and white does emphasize something which is here, but it emphasizes, or perhaps exaggerates it and therefore makes us put people together in groups which they ought not to be in. I have more in common with a black scholar than I have with a white man who is against scholarship. And you have* *more in common with a white author than you have with someone who is against all literature. So why must we always concentrate on color? Or religion? Or this? There are other ways of connecting men.*

JAMES BALDWIN: *I'll tell you this: when I left this country in 1948, I left this country for one reason only, one reason—I didn't care where I went. I might've gone to Hong Kong, I might have gone to Timbuktu. I ended up in Paris, on the streets of Paris, with forty dollars in my pocket on the theory that nothing worse could happen to me there than had already happened to me here. You talk about making it as a writer by yourself, you have to be able then to turn off all the antennae with which you live, because once you turn your back on this society you may die. You may die. And it's very hard to sit at a typewriter and concentrate on that if you are afraid of the world around you. The years I lived in Paris did one thing for me: they released me from that particular social terror, which was not the paranoia of my own mind, but a real social danger visible in the face of every cop, every boss, everybody.*

PAUL WEISS: *Not all . . .*

JAMES BALDWIN: *I don't know what most white people in this country feel. But I can only conclude what they feel from the state of their institutions. I don't know if white Christians hate Negroes or not, but I know we have a Christian church which is white and a Christian church which is black. I know, as Malcolm X once put it, the most segregated hour in American life is high noon on Sunday. That says a great deal for me about a Christian nation. It means I can't afford to trust most white Christians, and I* *certainly cannot trust the Christian church. I don't know whether the labor unions and their bosses really hate me—that doesn't matter—but I know I'm not in their union. I don't know whether the real estate lobby has anything against black people, but I know the real estate lobby is keeping me in the ghetto. I don't know if the board of education hates black people, but I know the textbooks they give my children to read and the schools we have to go to. Now, this is the evidence. You want me to make an act of faith, risking myself, my wife, my woman, my sister, my children on some idealism which you assure me exists in America, which I have never seen.*

All of the Western nations have been caught in a lie,
the lie of their pretended humanism;
this means that their history
has no moral justification,
and that the West has no moral authority.

"Vile as I am," states one of the characters
in Dostoyevsky's *The Idiot*,
"I don't believe in the wagons that bring bread
to humanity. For the wagons that bring bread
to humanity . . . may coldly exclude a considerable
part of humanity from enjoying what is brought."

For a very long time, America prospered:
this prosperity cost millions of people their lives.
Now, not even the people who are the most
spectacular recipients of the benefits of this
prosperity are able to endure these benefits:
they can neither understand them
nor do without them.
Above all, they cannot imagine the price paid
by their victims, or subjects, for this way of life,
and so they cannot afford to know
why the victims are revolting.

This is a formula for a nation's or a kingdom's
decline, for no kingdom can maintain
itself by force alone.

Force does not work the way
its advocates think in fact it does.
It does not, for example, reveal to the victim
the strength of the adversary.
On the contrary, it reveals the weakness,
even the panic of the adversary
and this revelation invests the victim with patience.

There is a day in Palm Springs
that I will remember forever,
a bright day.

I was based in Hollywood, working on the
screen version of *The Autobiography of Malcolm X*.
This was a difficult assignment, since I had known
Malcolm, after all, crossed swords with him,
worked with him, and held him in that great
esteem which is not easily distinguishable,
if it is distinguishable, from love.

Billy Dee Williams had come to town,
and he was staying at the house.
I very much wanted Billy Dee
for the role of Malcolm.

The phone had been brought out to the pool,
and now it rang.
And I picked it up.
The record player was still playing.

"He's not dead yet, but it's a head wound."

ROBERT KENNEDY: *I have some very sad news for all of you and I think sad news for all of our fellow citizens and people who love peace all over the world. And that is that Martin Luther King was shot and was killed tonight.*

I hardly remember the rest of the evening at all.
I remember weeping, briefly,
more in helpless rage than in sorrow,
and Billy trying to comfort me.
But I really don't remember that evening at all.

The church was packed.
In the pew before me sat Marlon Brando,
Sammy Davis, Eartha Kitt. Sidney Poitier nearby.

I saw Harry Belafonte sitting next to Coretta King.
I have a childhood hangover thing
about not weeping in public,

and I was concentrating on holding myself together.
I did not want to weep for Martin;
tears seemed futile.
But I may also have been afraid,
and I could not have been the only one,
that if I began to weep, I would not be able to stop.
I started to cry, and I stumbled.
Sammy grabbed my arm.

The story of the Negro in America
is the story of America.
It is not a pretty story.

What can we do?
Well, I am tired. . . .
I don't know how it will come about.
I know that no matter how it comes about,
it will be bloody;
it will be hard.
I still believe that we can do with this country
something that has not been done before.
We are misled here because we think of numbers.

You don't need numbers; you need passion.

And this is proven by the history of the world.
The tragedy is that most of the people
who say they care about it do not care.
What they care about is their safety and their profits.

The American way of life has failed—
to make people happier or make them better.
We do not want to admit this,
and we do not admit it.
We persist in believing that
the empty and criminal among our children

are the result of some miscalculation
in the formula that can be corrected;
that the bottomless and aimless hostility
which makes our cities among the most dangerous
in the world is created, and felt,
by a handful of aberrants;
that the lack, yawning everywhere in this country,
of passionate conviction, of personal authority,
proves only our rather appealing tendency
to be gregarious and democratic.

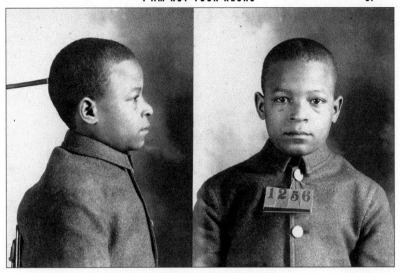

To look around the United States today
is enough to make prophets and angels weep.
This is not the land of the free;
it is only very unwillingly and sporadically
the home of the brave.

I sometimes feel it to be an absolute miracle
that the entire black population of the United States
of America has not long ago
succumbed to raging paranoia.
People finally say to you,
in an attempt to dismiss the social reality,
"But you're so bitter!"
Well, I may or may not be bitter,
but if I were, I would have good reasons for it:
chief among them that American blindness,
or cowardice, which allows us to pretend
that life presents no reasons for being bitter.

In this country,
for a dangerously long time,
there have been two levels of experience.
One, to put it cruelly, can be summed up
in the images of Gary Cooper and Doris Day:
two of the most grotesque appeals
to innocence the world has ever seen.
And the other,
subterranean, indispensable, and denied,
can be summed up, let us say,
in the tone and in the face of Ray Charles.

RAY CHARLES, "WHAT'D I SAY"

Hey mama, don't you treat me wrong
Come and love your daddy all night long
All right, all is right now, I know it's all right, hey hey hey
When you see me in misery
Come on baby, see about me.

And there has never been any genuine confrontation between these two levels of experience.

DORIS DAY, "SHOULD I SURRENDER"
FROM *LOVER COME BACK* - 1961 -

Should I be bad or nice?
Should I surrender?
His pleading words so tenderly entreat me.
Is this the night that love finally defeats me?

You cannot lynch me
and keep me in ghettos
without becoming something monstrous yourselves.
And furthermore, you give me a terrifying advantage.

You never had to look at me.
I had to look at you.
I know more about you than you know about me.
Not everything that is faced can be changed;
but nothing can be changed until it is faced.

History is not the past.
It is the present.
We carry our history with us.
We *are* our history.
If we pretend otherwise, we literally are criminals.

I attest to this:
the world is not white;
it never was white,
cannot be white.
White is a metaphor for power,
and that is simply a way of describing
Chase Manhattan Bank.

THE NEGRO AND THE AMERICAN PROMISE - 1963 -

JAMES BALDWIN: *I can't be a pessimist, because I'm alive. To be a pessimist means you have agreed that human life is an academic matter, so I'm forced to be an optimist. I'm forced to believe that we can survive whatever we must survive. But the Negro in this country . . . the future of the Negro in this country is precisely as bright or as dark as the future of the country. It is entirely up to the American people and our representatives—it is entirely up to the American people whether or not they are going to face and deal with and embrace this stranger who they have maligned so long. What white people have to do is try and find out in their own*

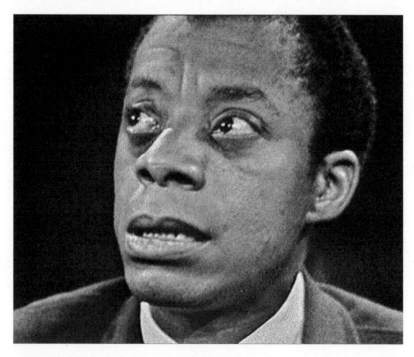

hearts why it was necessary to have a "nigger" in the first place, because I'm not a nigger, I'm a man. But if you think I'm a nigger, it means you need him. The question that you've got to ask yourself, the white population of this country has got to ask itself, North and South because it's one country and for a Negro there is no difference between the North and the South—it's just a difference in the way they castrate you, but the fact of the castration is the American fact. . . . If I'm not the nigger here and you invented him, you the white people invented him, then you've got to find out why. And the future of the country depends on that, whether or not it is able to ask that question.

CREDITS

I AM NOT YOUR NEGRO
(93 min. USA/France/Belgium/Switzerland)

Directed by Raoul Peck
Written by James Baldwin,
   compiled and edited by Raoul Peck
Narrated by Samuel L. Jackson

Producers: Rémi Grellety, Raoul Peck, Hébert Peck
Coproducers: Patrick Quinet, Joëlle Bertossa
With the full support and collaboration
   of the James Baldwin Estate

Editor: Alexandra Strauss
Cinematography: Henry Adebonojo, Bill Ross,
   Turner Ross
Animator: Michel Blustein
Sound: Valérie Le Docte, David Gillain
Music: Alexei Aigui
Archival research: Marie-Hélène Barbéris,
   assisted by Nolwenn Gouault

ARTE France: Fabrice Puchault, Alex Szalat
Executive Producers for ITVS: Sally Jo Fifer, Lois Vossen
Executive Producer for NBPC: Leslie Fields-Cruz

Produced by Velvet Film, Inc. (USA), Velvet Film (France), Artémis Productions, Close Up Films
In coproduction with ARTE France, Independent Television Service (ITVS) with funding provided by the Corporation for Public Broadcasting (CPB), RTS Radio Télévision Suisse, RTBF (Télévision belge), Shelter Prod
With the support of Centre National du Cinéma et de l'Image Animée, MEDIA Programme of the European Union, Sundance Institute Documentary Film Program, National Black Programming Consortium (NBPC), Cinereach, PROCIREP—Société des Producteurs, ANGOA, Taxshelter.be, ING, Tax Shelter Incentive of the Federal Government of Belgium, Cinéforom, Loterie Romande

Sales Agents: ICM Partners, Wide House

BIBLIOGRAPHY

James Baldwin's works used for the narration of *I Am Not Your Negro*:

"As Much Truth As One Can Bear." *New York Times Book Review*, January 14, 1962. Collected in *The Cross of Redemption*.

"Black English: A Dishonest Argument." In *Black English and the Education of Black Children and Youth: Proceedings of the National Invitational Symposium on the King Decision*. Detroit: Center for Black Studies, Wayne State University, 1980. Collected in *The Cross of Redemption*.

The Cross of Redemption. New York: Pantheon Books, 2010.

The Devil Finds Work. New York: Vintage Books, 1976, 2011.

Letter from James Baldwin to Jay Acton, June 30, 1979. In "Notes Toward Remember This House," October 28, 1980.

"Lorraine Hansberry at the Summit." *Freedomways*, no. 19 (1979): 269–72. Collected in *The Cross of Redemption*.

"Mass Culture and the Creative Artist: Some Personal Notes." In *Culture for the Millions: Mass Media in Modern Society*, edited by Norman Jacobs. Princeton, N. J.: Van Nostrand, 1959. Collected in *The Cross of Redemption*.

From *Nationalism, Colonialism, and the United States: One Minute to 12!* A Forum Sponsored by the Liberation Committee for Africa on Its First Anniversary Celebration, June 2, 1961. New York: Photo-Offset Press, 1961. Collected in *The Cross of Redemption*.

"The News from All the Northern Cities Is, to Understate It, Grim; the State of the Union Is Catastrophic." *New York Times*, April 5, 1978. Collected in *The Cross of Redemption*.

No Name in the Street. New York: Vintage Books, 1972.

"Sidney Poitier." *Look*, July 23, 1968. Collected in *The Cross of Redemption*.

"The White Problem." In *100 Years of Emancipation*, edited by Robert A. Goodwin. Chicago: Rand McNally, 1964. Collected in *The Cross of Redemption*.

PERMISSIONS

ILLUSTRATIONS